The Everglades

Lisa Bullard

Lerner Publications Company
Minneapolis

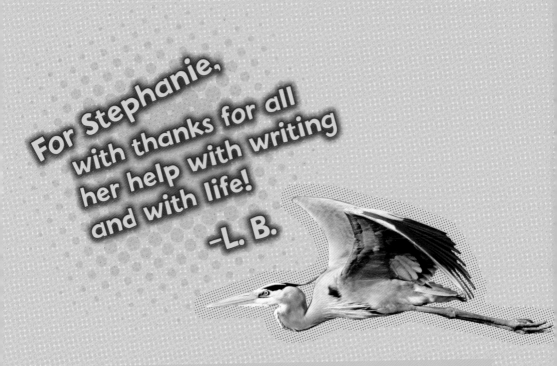

For Stephanie,
with thanks for all
her help with writing
and with life!
—L. B.

Lerner Publications Company
A division of Lerner Publishing Group, Inc.
241 First Avenue North
Minneapolis, MN 55401 USA

For reading levels and more information, look up this title at www.lernerbooks.com.

Library of Congress Cataloging-in-Publication Data

Bullard, Lisa.
    The Everglades — by Lisa Bullard.
        p.   cm. — (Lightning bolt books™—Famous places)
    Includes index.
    ISBN 978-0-7613-4453-7 (lib. bdg. : alk. paper)
    ISBN 978-0-7613-5958-6 (eBook)
    1. Everglades (Fla.)—Juvenile literature. 2. Everglades National Park (Fla.)—
Juvenile literature. I. Title.
    F317.E9B85 2010
    975.9′39—dc22   2009016902

Manufactured in the United States of America
1-48209-48777-9/19/2019

Contents

Welcome to the Everglades

Have you ever seen this place? It is the Everglades.

The Everglades is a giant wetland in southern Florida.

The Everglades is home to many plants and animals. These plants and animals do not live together anywhere else on Earth.

Two spoonbills rest on the end of a branch.

The Everglades is also important for humans. It provides clean water for Florida's people and farms.

Farmers in southern Florida need water for their crops.

Water, Water Everywhere

There are only two seasons in the Everglades. Can you guess what they are?

An alligator stays cool in a pool of water during the warm, dry winter months.

They are winter and summer!

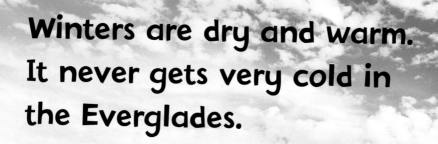

Winters are dry and warm. It never gets very cold in the Everglades.

Plants can turn dry and brown during the winter in the Everglades.

9

Rain pours down on the Everglades during a summer rainstorm.

Summers are wet and hot. It rains about 60 inches (152 centimeters) each year. The rain floods the land.

Much of the Everglades is low and flat. The low, flat areas are called freshwater marshes. They are underwater for many months each year.

The Everglades' freshwater marshes are underwater much of the time.

Sloughs are paths for moving water. The water moves in a wide, slow river.

Plant Life

Saw grass is a tall plant. It grows in marshes. Saw grass leaves have cutting edges like a saw. They can cut people's skin.

An egret flies beside some tall saw grass.

Cypress trees can survive with the bottom parts of their trunks underwater.

Cypress trees can grow in freshwater.

Other trees grow where it is higher and drier. Some of these areas are called tree islands.

Trees grow in a clump where the land is higher.

Smoke billows from a
fire in the Everglades.

Some dry areas are covered
with pine trees. Lightning
strikes can start fires there.

Freshwater mixes with salty ocean water at Florida's southern tip. Mangrove trees grow well in this salty water.

Mangrove roots provide homes for small water creatures.

Animal Life

Many animals make their homes in the Everglades. Can you guess the most common?

Insects! Insects love this wet world.

Alligators are also important to the Everglades. They dig holes called gator holes that fill with water. Fish survive dry times in gator holes.

Large wading
birds like the
great blue
heron look for
food in the water.
More than 350
kinds of birds live
in the Everglades.

Mammals such as the Florida panther live there too.

Many water animals make the Everglades their home. Manatees look for plants to eat in shallow water.

A manatee swims through the murky waters of the Everglades.

The Changing Everglades

The Everglades used to cover most of southern Florida. But the Everglades is about half its former size.

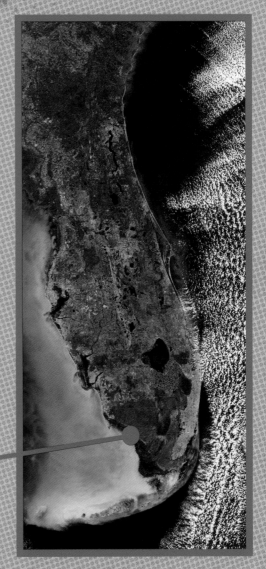

The greenish brown area in this picture is the Everglades. The Everglades once covered much more of Florida's land.

People built farms and homes in the Everglades.

They changed the path of the water.

Homes such as these can be found in the Everglades. This picture was taken from an airplane.

Some of the Everglades is still mostly wild. But these parts are in danger too. There is too little water and too much pollution.

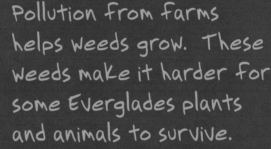

Pollution from farms helps weeds grow. These weeds make it harder for some Everglades plants and animals to survive.

People understand the importance of the Everglades. It provides clean water for Florida's people. It is home to many plants and animals.

These workers are trying to protect Florida panthers that live in the Everglades.

People are working to save the Everglades. They are fighting to bring back more wild wetland.

The Everglades Area

ALABAMA

GEORGIA

FLORIDA

Gulf of Mexico

CANADA

UNITED STATES

PACIFIC OCEAN

ATLANTIC OCEAN

Everglades

Florida

MEXICO

Gulf of Mexico

UNITED STATES

Florida

N

Everglades

Everglades National Park

Miles

0   20   40   60   80

0   40   80   120

Kilometers

Fun Facts

- Marjory Stoneman Douglas was an early protector of the Everglades. She called the area a river of grass. This has become a famous nickname for the Everglades.

- Hurricanes are dangerous storms with strong winds and rain. They sometimes pass over the Everglades in the summer. Hurricanes help shape the Everglades. Their strong winds blow down trees. Hurricanes also spread seeds so that plants can grow in new places.

- Saw grass leaves burn when fire crosses the Everglades. But their roots are protected by water. The plants grow back quickly.

- Many of the animals in the Everglades are at risk. Florida panthers, wood storks, manatees, and American crocodiles are hard to find. People are working hard to make sure these animals don't disappear.

Glossary

freshwater: water that does not contain salt

mammal: an animal that has hair, drinks its mother's milk, and whose body heat always stays about the same

marsh: an area of wet, low land

pollution: something that gets into air, land, or water and makes it dirty

saw grass: a tall plant that grows in marshes. Its leaves have cutting edges like a saw.

slough: a path for moving water

wetland: a land area in which there is much moisture in the soil

Further Reading

Florida Department of Environmental Protection Kid's Page
http://www.dep.state.fl.us/secretary/kids

Johnson, Rebecca L. *A Journey into a Wetland.* Minneapolis: Lerner Publications Company, 2004.

Leotti-Bachem, Janice. *Everglades.* New York: Children's Press, 2005.

National Geographic Explorer: Exploring the Everglades
http://magma.nationalgeographic.com/ngexplorer/0504/games/game_intro.html

U.S. Geological Survey's South Florida Information Access Kid's Page
http://sofia.usgs.gov/virtual_tour/kids

Yolen, Jane. *Welcome to the River of Grass.* New York: Putnam, 2001.

Index

Photo Acknowledgments

The images in this book are used with the permission of: © FloridaStock/Shutterstock Images, pp. 2, 6, 30; © Jim Wark/Lonely Planet Images/Getty Images, pp. 4–5; © Bob Gibbons/Photoshot, p. 7; © Tim Chapman/Liason/Getty Images, p. 8; © Fergus O'Brien/ Taxi/Getty Images, p. 9; © Wallece Weeks/Alamy, p. 10; © Peter Horree/Alamy, p. 11; © Imagebroker.com/Photoshot, p. 12; © Jeff Greenberg/World Illustrated/Photoshot, p. 13; © Farrell Grehan/National Geographic/Getty Images, p. 14; © James Randkiev/ Photographer's Choice/Getty Images, p. 15; © Otis Imboden/National Geographic/Getty Images, p. 16; © Raul Touzon/National Geographic/Getty Images, p. 17; © Joe Austin Photography/Alamy, p. 18 (left); © Stephen Dalton/NHPA/Photoshot, p. 18 (top right, bottom right); © James D. Watt/Stephen Frink Collection/Alamy, p. 19; © Jeff Foot/ Discovery Channel Images/Getty Images, p. 20; © James Carmichael Jr/NHPA/ Photoshot, p. 21; © Wayne Johnson/Shutterstock Images, p. 22; Visible Earth/NASA, p. 23; © James P. Blair/National Geographic/Getty Images, p. 24; © William F. Campbell/Time & Life Pictures/Getty Images, p. 25; U.S. Fish and Wildlife Service, p. 26; © Rich Reid/National Geographic/Getty Images, p. 27; © Laura Westlund/Independent Picture Service, p. 28; © Renaud Visage/Photographer's Choice/Getty Images, p. 31.

Front cover: © FloridaStock/Shutterstock Images, (heron); © altrendo nature/Getty Images (landscape, alligator).

Do you know a place that's home to both manatees and panthers? Get ready for a trip to the Everglades! Many plants and animals live in this huge wetland. But why is the Everglades region also important to humans? And how do people protect the Everglades? Read this book to find out!

Learn about many remarkable sites in the Famous Places series—part of the Lightning Bolt Books™ collection. With high-energy designs, exciting photos, and fun text, Lightning Bolt Books™ bring nonfiction topics to life!

Famous Places

The Alamo

The Capitol Building

The Empire State Building

The Erie Canal

The Everglades

The Gateway Arch

The Golden Gate Bridge

The Grand Canyon

The Great Lakes

The Hoover Dam

The Lincoln Memorial

Mount Rushmore

The Redwood Forests

The Rocky Mountains

The Statue of Liberty

The Washington Monument

The White House

Yellowstone National Park

ISBN 978-1-5415-9935-2

LernerClassroom™
A division of Lerner Publishing Group
www.lernerbooks.com
005–008 ATOS: 3.2 Lexile: 590
Guided Reading: M

9 781541 599352